These Are Strange Times

A Journal/Activity Book for Kids
Ages 6 to 10
(or for the kid in all of us!)

THIS JOURNAL BELONGS TO

_____

Dear Young Friend,

Your life is probably very different now from what it was just a little while ago. Here is a journal in which you can write about who you are, what you like (and don't like), and some of the things that are going on in your life right now.

This is not a homework assignment, so you can spend as much, or as little, time on it as you want. It's not a test, either, so you can ask for help any time you want. The most important thing? Just have fun with it.

When you're finished, and after these crazy days have passed, this journal might be something you'll want to reread once in a while. And, who knows? Maybe one day you'll even want to show it to your children or grandchildren and tell them what your life was like during these strange times.

If you're ready, then turn the page ...

Let's Start with When You Were Born (Because, Really, Does It Matter What the World Was Like Before You Got Here?)

Write your whole name on the line below.

_____

Do you have a nickname?

_____

What is your birthday?

_____

What time of day were you born?

_____

What day of the week was it?

_____

How much did you weigh?

_____

How tall were you?

_____

Where were you born?

_____

Was it in a hospital? At home? On a bus?

_____

Does your mom or dad remember what the weather was like on that day?

_____

_____

Do you know anything about what was happening in the world on the day you were born? (Maybe your parents can tell you.)

_____

_____

_____

_____

_____

_____

_____

Take a break.
Write, draw, or doodle
anything you want on this page.

It Really Is a Small World ...

Where do you live?

_____

_____

How long have you lived there?

_____

Where else have you lived?

_____

_____

_____

Who do you live with? What are their names?

_____

_____

_____

_____

_____

_____

Draw a picture of your family.

Do you have any pets? What are their names?

_____

_____

_____

_____

_____

If you could have any pet you want, real or imagined, what would it be?

_____

_____

_____

_____

_____

If you were an animal, what would you be? Why?

_____

_____

_____

_____

_____

What is your favorite story about your family, your pet(s), or your neighborhood?

_____

_____

_____

_____

_____

_____

_____

_____

_____

_____

_____

_____

_____

_____

_____

_____

_____

_____

Draw a picture of your favorite pet or yourself as an animal!

School Is In . . . School Is Out?

What's the name of your school?

_____

_____

Where is it?

_____

What grade are you in?

_____

What do you like most about your school?

_____

_____

_____

_____

_____

_____

_____

Who is your teacher?

_____

What do you like most about your teacher?

_____

_____

_____

_____

_____

_____

What is your favorite subject? (And, no, you're not allowed to say "recess"!)

_____

_____

_____

_____

_____

_____

Have you gone to any other schools?

_____

_____

_____

_____

_____

What has been your favorite school so far? Why?

_____

_____

_____

_____

_____

Who has been your favorite teacher so far? Why?

_____

_____

_____

_____

_____

Take a break.
Solve these Word Scrambles.
(Hint: They're all school-related.)

S   A   L   S   C

___ ___ ___ ___ ___

Y   A   I   R   R   L   B

___ ___ ___ ___ ___ ___ ___

E   S   R   E   C   S

___ ___ ___ ___ ___ ___

H   E   E   C   R   T   A

___ ___ ___ ___ ___ ___ ___

You'll find the answers on page 44.

It's All About You (Well, Actually, Not <u>All</u>)

Who are your best friends? What's "best" about them?

_____

_____

_____

_____

_____

_____

_____

_____

_____

_____

_____

_____

_____

_____

_____

_____

_____

Do you have a hero? Who is it? Why? (P.S. It can be more than one person, real or imagined.)

_____

_____

_____

_____

If you could have a super power, what would it be? How would you use it?

_____

_____

_____

_____

_____

_____

Do you have a favorite toy? More than one?

_____

_____

_____

_____

Do you like to listen to music? What kind?

_____

_____

_____

_____

_____

_____

_____

Do you play a musical instrument? Is there one you want to learn to play?

_____

_____

_____

_____

_____

_____

_____

What kinds of things do you like to read about?

_____

_____

_____

_____

_____

_____

_____

_____

What is your favorite book? Who wrote it? Why is it your favorite?

_____

_____

_____

_____

_____

_____

_____

_____

Do you like video games? What are your favorites?

_____

_____

_____

_____

_____

If you watch TV, what are your favorite shows?

_____

_____

_____

_____

_____

What are your favorite movies?

_____

_____

_____

_____

_____

Do you play any sports? What are your favorite sports and teams?

_____

_____

_____

_____

_____

_____

_____

_____

Do you have any hobbies?

_____

_____

_____

_____

_____

_____

_____

If you could eat your favorite foods for the whole day, what would they be?

For Breakfast:

_____

_____

_____

_____

For Lunch:

_____

_____

_____

_____

For Dinner:

_____

_____

_____

_____

Write about some of your favorite things to do, like playing video games or drawing. What's fun about them?

_____

_____

_____

_____

_____

_____

_____

_____

_____

_____

_____

_____

_____

_____

_____

_____

Take a break.
Play a few games of Tic Tac Toe
with someone.

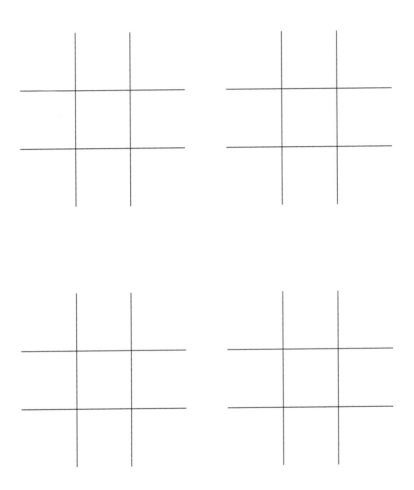

My Life These Days ...

Think about how much your life has recently changed. There have been a lot of changes, and they happened pretty fast, didn't they? What's different about your life now? What do you miss most? Maybe it's seeing your friends at school, visiting with your grandparents, or going to your church, synagogue, or mosque.

_____

_____

_____

_____

_____

_____

_____

_____

_____

_____

_____

_____

_____

What is a "normal" day like for you now?

_____

_____

_____

_____

_____

_____

_____

_____

_____

_____

_____

_____

_____

_____

_____

_____

How do you feel about the changes to your days? What are some good things about them? What don't you like so much?

_____

_____

_____

_____

_____

_____

_____

_____

_____

_____

_____

_____

_____

_____

_____

How can you help make things better for yourself?
Maybe you want to talk to your mom or dad about
this question.

_____

_____

_____

_____

_____

_____

_____

How can you help make things better for someone
else? Maybe you want to ask your mom or dad about
this question.

_____

_____

_____

_____

_____

_____

_____

Is there anything new that you like to do but didn't have time to do before?

_____

_____

_____

_____

_____

_____

_____

_____

_____

_____

_____

_____

_____

_____

Take a break.
Play Connect the Dots with someone.

How to play:

1. The game has two players.

2. You take turns drawing lines between two dots, either up and down or across.

3. If you draw the fourth line of a box, initial inside it, and draw another line. (If the other line you draw also completes a box, you keep going until the line you draw isn't the fourth line and doesn't complete a box.)

4. The player who completes the most boxes wins.

Who Knows What Tomorrow Will Bring?

What's today's date? _____

What do you think your life will be like in three months?

_____

_____

_____

_____

_____

_____

What do you think your life will be like in six months?

_____

_____

_____

_____

_____

_____

What do you think your life will be like a year from now? What grade will you be in? What will school be like? Will you have the same friends? Will you have new friends? Will you have any new hobbies?

_____

_____

_____

_____

_____

_____

_____

_____

_____

_____

_____

_____

_____

_____

Take a break.
Using the letters in each word below,
form as many new words as you can.

S U N S E T

G A R D E N

M O U N T A I N

You'll find the answers on page 44.

The Future Is Yours . . .

Are you excited for the future? Maybe a little nervous?
Write about that.

_____

_____

_____

_____

_____

_____

_____

_____

_____

_____

_____

_____

_____

_____

If you could go anywhere in the world you wanted to, where would that be? Why? Would you want to live there or just visit?

_____

_____

_____

_____

_____

_____

_____

_____

_____

_____

_____

_____

_____

_____

_____

_____

Do you ever think about what you want to be when you grow up? What kind of person will you be? What will you do for a job? Will you have a family?

_____

_____

_____

_____

_____

_____

_____

_____

_____

_____

_____

_____

_____

_____

_____

Take a break.
Last chance ... write, draw, or doodle
whatever you want on this page.

Write a story. Any story. It can be true. It can be made up. It can be about anything you want. Illustrate it in the margins if you want.

Almost finished ...
Do you have any special photos
you want to tape onto the next few pages?

You've finished the chapters of this journal. Well done. But this is just the start—your life has many more exciting chapters to come!

Answers to Word Scramble:

CLASS   LIBRARY   RECESS   TEACHER

Answers to Word Game:

Garden

are	dare	dear	den	drag
ear	gear	grad	grade	nag
near	rag	rage	ran	read
red				

Mountain

an	at	in	main	mat
mint	moan	mount	nit	no
not	noun	nun	nut	oat
on	out	tan	tin	ton

Weather

are	at	ate	ear	eat
he	hear	heat	her	here
raw	tea	tear	thaw	the
there	three	threw	tree	wart
water	we	wear	wet	what
wheat	wreath			

ISBN: 9798642280737